DOCUMENTING HISTORY

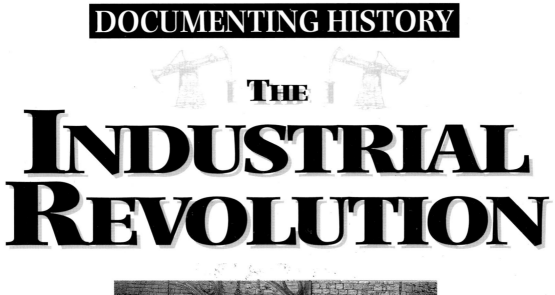

The
INDUSTRIAL
REVOLUTION

STEWART ROSS

FRANKLIN WATTS
A Division of Scholastic Inc.
NEW YORK TORONTO LONDON AUCKLAND SYDNEY

MEXICO CITY NEW DELHI HONG KONG

DANBURY, CONNECTICUT

First published by Evans Brothers Limited, 2000
2A Portman Mansions
Chiltern Street
London
W1M 1LE

© Evans Brothers Limited 2000

First American edition 2001 by Franklin Watts
A Division of Scholastic Inc.
90 Sherman Turnpike
Danbury, CT 06816

Catalog details are available from the Library of Congress
Cataloging-in-Publication Data

Printed in Spain by GRAFO

ISBN 0-531-14609-X (Lib. Bdg.)

Design – Neil Sayer
Editorial – Nicola Barber
Maps – Tim Smith
Consultant – John Powell, Ironbridge Gorge Museum
Production – Jenny Mulvanny

Title page picture: Workers at a dock, an engraving by Gustave Doré

ACKNOWLEDGMENTS

For permission to reproduce copyright pictorial material, the author and publishers gratefully acknowledge the following:

Cover (top left and right) Mary Evans Picture Library (bottom left) Bridgeman Art Library (bottom right) Mary Evans Picture Library **title page** Mary Evans Picture Library **page 7** (top right) Ironbridge Gorge Museum (bottom) Scottish National Portrait Gallery, Edinburgh/Bridgeman Art Library, London/New York **page 8** Chateau de Malmaison, Paris/Roger-Viollet, Paris/Bridgeman Art Library **page 9** (top) Private Collection/Bridgeman Art Library (bottom) Mary Evans Picture Library **page 10** Mary Evans Picture Library **page 11** City of Edinburgh Museums and Art Galleries/Bridgeman Art Library **page 12** (top) British Library/Bridgeman Art Library (bottom) Guildhall Library, Corporation of London/Bridgeman Art Library **page 13** Mary Evans Picture Library **page 14** Private Collection/Bridgeman Art Library **page 15** (left) British Library (right) Mary Evans Picture Library **page 16** Mary Evans Picture Library **page 17** Guildhall Library, Corporation of London/Bridgeman Art Library **page 18** Christie's Images, London/Bridgeman Art Library **page 19** British Museum, London/Bridgeman Art Library **page 20** British Library/Bridgeman Art Library **page 21** Mary Evans Picture Library **page 22** Mary Evans Picture Library **page 23** Private Collection/Bridgeman Art Library **page 24** Mary Evans Picture Library **page 25** (left) Mary Evans Picture Library (right) Mary Evans Picture Library **page 26** Walker Art Gallery, Liverpool/Board of Trustees: National Museums and Galleries on Merseyside/Bridgeman Art Library **page 27** (top) Ironbridge Gorge Museum, Telford/Bridgeman Art Library (bottom right) Ironbridge Gorge Museum **page 28** Guildhall Library, Corporation of London/Bridgeman Art Library **page 29** Hulton Getty **page 30** Mary Evans Picture Library **page 31** (top) Mary Evans Picture Library (bottom) Mary Evans Picture Library **page 32** Mary Evans Picture Library **page 33** Mary Evans Picture Library **page 34** Guildhall Library, Corporation of London/Bridgeman Art Library **page 35** (top) Bettmann/Hulton Getty (bottom) Mary Evans Picture Library **page 36** (top) Mary Evans Picture Library (bottom) National Railway Museum, York/Bridgeman Art Library **page 37** Mary Evans Picture Library **page 38** Mary Evans Picture Library **page 39** (top) Mary Evans Picture Library (bottom) Mary Evans Picture Library **page 40** Mary Evans Picture Library **page 41** (left) Mary Evans Picture Library (right) Mary Evans Picture Library **page 42** (top) Mary Evans Picture Library (bottom) Mary Evans Picture Library **page 43** (left) Mary Evans Picture Library (right) British Library **page 44** City of Bristol Museum and Art Gallery/Bridgeman Art Library **page 45** (top left) Mary Evans Picture Library (middle right) Private Collection/Bridgeman Art Library **page 46** Mary Evans Picture Library **page 47** (top) Mary Evans Picture Library (bottom) Mary Evans Picture Library **page 49** The Illustrated London News Picture Library/Bridgeman Art Library **page 50** Museum of the City of New York, USA/Bridgeman Art Library **page 51** (top) Mary Evans Picture Library (bottom) Scottish National Portrait Gallery, Edinburgh/Bridgeman Art Library **page 52** (top) Mary Evans Picture Library (bottom) Mary Evans Picture Library **page 53** Private Collection/Bridgeman Art Library **page 54** (top) Mary Evans Picture Library (bottom) Mary Evans Picture Library **page 55** Private Collection/Bridgeman Art Library **page 56** Private Collection/Bridgeman Art Library **page 57** (left) JHC Wilson/Robert Harding Picture Library (right) Trip/Ask Images

CONTENTS

CHAPTER 1

INTRODUCTION

LOOKING AT DOCUMENTS

The Industrial Revolution changed the world. This book explains what the Revolution was, how it began, and how it affected millions of lives. The first chapters focus on Britain, which for a time was at the center of the Industrial Revolution. Even so, from the beginning the Revolution was an international movement, involving trade in materials and goods between countries such as the United States, Germany, Russia, and Japan. Later chapters examine how manufacturing grew up outside Britain and helped create a modern industrial world.

This book brings the remarkable story of the Industrial Revolution alive through documents written at the time the Revolution was actually happening. These include newspaper articles, letters, government reports, satirical cartoons, and comments by politicians, writers, and business people. There are even a few angry pieces by those who hated the Revolution. To make the documents easier to read, we have printed them in modern type. You will also find photographs of some of the original documents, so you can see what they looked like. Difficult or old-fashioned language is explained next to the document itself.

A document can be misleading. Its meaning and importance are not always obvious at first. So, when looking at one of the documents printed in this book, you need to ask yourself three important questions. First, when was the document written? The answer will allow you to work out what was going on at the time. Second, who wrote it? You need to know this in order to understand the point of view of the writer. For example, consider the use of the word "poor." In the early 19th century a nobleman might have described himself as "poor" if he had $750 a year. But factory workers earning $750 a year would have thought themselves rich. Third, why was the document written? Was the writer trying to offer unbiased facts, or was he or she arguing a case? Like a detective, you need to examine the evidence very carefully.

Here are four excerpts from documents found in the book. They give an idea of the wide variety of sources used. Each document has an introduction explaining how and why it was written.

 Some writers, such as Friedrich Engels, concentrated on the worst consequences of the Industrial Revolution (see page 23).

The cottages are old, dirty, and of the smallest sort, the streets uneven, fallen into ruts and in part without drains or pavement; masses of refuse, offal and sickening filth lie among standing pools in all directions.

A QUESTION OF LANGUAGE
Most of the documents are printed using the words and phrases as they were first written. A few spellings have been modernized. Three dots (...) show where some of the original words have been left out. This has been done to make the document shorter or easier to understand.

This original document gives you some information about how a major construction project was organized in the 1770s. It is an estimate for the costs of materials for the world's first iron bridge (see page 27) and a list of the people prepared to put up money to pay for the bridge.

This estimate for erecting a cast iron bridge (with stone abutments) over the River Severn between Madeley & Broseley.

Other documents are official reports. They use official language and try to give an unbiased account of the facts, like this one (see page 13).

580 towns were distinguished in 1851, and the population in them and in the surrounding country was nearly equal.

Advice like this from the American millionaire Andrew Carnegie (see page 51) helps to capture the mood of the times.

Assuming that you have obtained employment and are fairly started, my advice to you is "aim high." I would not give a fig for the young man who does not already see himself the partner or the head of an important firm.

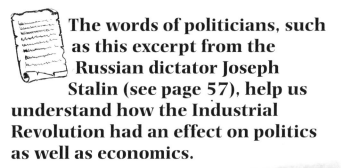

The words of politicians, such as this excerpt from the Russian dictator Joseph Stalin (see page 57), help us understand how the Industrial Revolution had an effect on politics as well as economics.

We are fifty or a hundred years behind the advanced countries. We must make good this distance in ten years. Either we do it, or they crush us.

WHAT REVOLUTION?

A revolution is a rapid, total, and permanent change. It usually refers to political change. Two well-known examples are the American Revolution (1775–83), which led to the foundation of the United States of America, and the French Revolution (1789–99), when France became a republic.

The Industrial Revolution is more difficult to define. The term describes a fairly quick change in the way things were made and sold, and how people lived and worked. This change involved the development of power-driven machinery, the use of money (or capital) in more complicated ways, the growth of towns, and improvements in transport. In other words, the phrase "Industrial Revolution" covers many different developments that all took place at the same time. (Some historians describe each of these changes as a revolution—for example, the Commercial Revolution, the Transport Revolution, and so on.)

There was no single Industrial Revolution. Different countries industrialized at different times and in different ways. The movement started in Britain, which is why the British Industrial Revolution is often referred to as *the* Industrial Revolution. By 1850 industrialization was taking root in parts of Western Europe and the United States, and by the end of the 19th century it had spread to Russia and Japan.

A highly romanticized portrayal of Emperor Napoleon Bonaparte by the French painter Jacques Louis David. Napoleon rose to power after the French Revolution, and images like this helped spread the idea that revolutions were noble and glorious.

This book looks at Britain's Industrial Revolution, then compares it with the countries that industrialized later on. Remember that the Industrial Revolution had no sudden beginning or end. Industrial change slowly gathered speed until, by about 1820, people were talking about a "revolution." By 1830 Britain was an industrial nation, making most of its money from manufacturing and commerce. One-third of its population lived in towns. Because the Industrial Revolution had no definite beginning or end, some people say it is a meaningless phrase. However, whatever we choose to call it, something remarkable and unique happened in Britain between about 1760 and 1830 and, in other countries, later.

Power loom weaving in 1834. Note the dangerously unfenced (unprotected) machinery.

THE POWER OF MONEY

The phrase "Industrial Revolution" was first used by a Frenchman, Louis Guillaume, in 1799. Guillaume, a diplomat in Berlin, used the expression because he believed that the industrial changes taking place in Britain were as far-reaching as the political changes of the recent French Revolution (1789–99). Like the French emperor Napoleon Bonaparte, who described the British as a "nation of shopkeepers," Guillaume was both fascinated and annoyed by the wealth provided by British industry and commerce. Backed by British money, a coalition of European nations eventually defeated France in the European wars that dragged on from 1793 to 1815.

In fact, England was already different from most countries. Even in 1700 a higher proportion of its wealth came from industry and commerce than in other countries.

In 1840 London's population was about two million. Historians question many of Engels's statistics.

Engels was eager to praise the working classes. He believed they would overthrow the government in a revolution.

When Friedrich Engels (1820–95), the son of a German textile manufacturer, came to England to look after his father's businesses, he was horrified by the conditions of working men and women. In the introduction to his book *The Condition of the Working Class in England* (1845), he set out his views on the changes that had happened in England over the previous 80 years.

Friedrich Engels

Sixty, eighty years ago, England was a country like every other, with small towns, few and simple industries, and a thin but proportionately large agricultural population. Today it is a country like no other, with a capital of two and a half million inhabitants; with vast manufacturing cities; with an industry that supplies the world, and produces almost everything by means of the most complex machinery; with an industrious, intelligent, dense population, of which two-thirds are employed in trade and commerce...

CHAPTER 2

WHY BRITAIN?

STABILITY

By the middle of the 18th century the British system of government was the envy of Europe. French philosophers held it up as a model for other nations to copy. The key to the system was balance. The events of the Glorious Revolution of 1688–89 (see box, page 11), when a Bill of Rights was passed through Parliament, had severely limited the power of British monarchs. Parliament controlled taxes and spending, and ministers of the Crown needed Parliament's support..

The power of the elected House of Commons was limited by the House of Lords, where the hereditary nobility sat. The art of government lay in balancing the wishes of the Crown, Commons, and Lords. By the time of Sir Robert Walpole (Britain's first prime minister, 1721–42), people were used to the idea of a loyal opposition—politicians who opposed the government but were nevertheless loyal to the Crown. In other words, they believed that policies could be challenged and changed without bringing the whole system down. This stability allowed merchants and manufacturers to plan for the future with confidence.

The House of Commons in the 18th century represented the families with money and land. It did not represent the majority of the people, who were not permitted to vote at elections. Consequently, governments tended to do what the landowners and merchants wanted. They kept taxes low and helped British commerce with measures such as the Navigation Acts, which reserved trade with Britain's colonies for British ships only. Anyone wanting to move goods around mainland Europe

Shown here are the members of the British House of Commons in the early 18th century.

This is a portrayal of Britain's last invader and leader of the Jacobites, Bonnie Prince Charlie, in Edinburgh, 1745.

faced many tolls and tariffs (taxes). However, after the union with Scotland (1707), there were no such tolls in Britain.

Although Britain was often at war, apart from the Jacobite rebellions (1715 and 1745; in support of the exiled House of Stuart), there was no fighting on home soil. This allowed merchants and manufacturers to get on with what they did best—making money. Wars could help British commerce, too. The Seven Years' War (1756–63), for example, left Britain as the major power in India and North America, opening up huge opportunities for British traders.

THE GLORIOUS REVOLUTION

In the 17th century, Crown and Parliament fought for power. In 1688, after almost 50 years of turmoil, the unpopular King James II was driven from the country. In his place, his daughter Mary and her husband William of Orange became king and queen. This event became known as the Glorious Revolution because it took place without bloodshed and had the backing of the majority of the people. After the Glorious Revolution, Crown and Parliament governed together. This new system of government lasted throughout most of the Industrial Revolution.

The historian Henry Hallam (1777–1859) believed the way Britain was governed was an important reason why the country was so prosperous. In 1818 he set out his views —rather pompously!—in his book *Europe During the Middle Ages*.

In fact, prosperity did not increase "uninterruptedly." During the wars against France, there were long periods of hardship.

Derives means "gets."

This refers to Parliament and the monarchy.

No unbiased observer, who derives pleasure from the welfare of his species, can fail to consider the long and uninterruptedly increasing prosperity of England as the most beautiful phenomenon in the history of mankind... in no other region have the benefits that political institutions can confer been diffused over so extended a population; nor have any people so well reconciled the discordant elements of wealth, order, and liberty.

Means "balanced the opposing forces of..."

Diffused means "spread."

MORE OF EVERYTHING

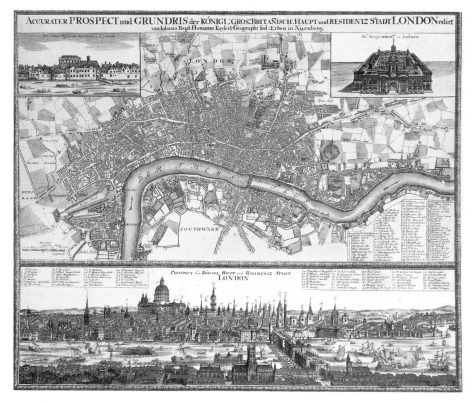

These two maps tell the story of the growth of London between 1730 (above) and 1850 (below). By 1850 the city's westward expansion had already swallowed up several country villages.

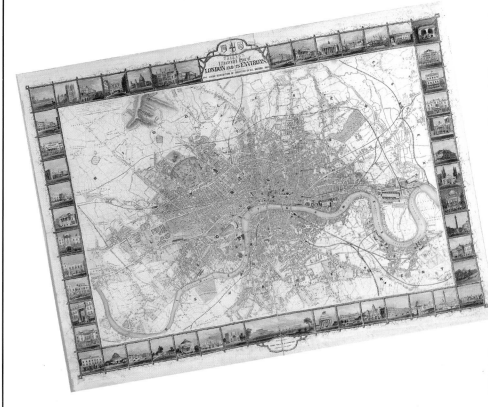

At the time of the Industrial Revolution, the British population was rising at a rate never experienced before. Nowadays, rapid population growth is nothing new, but before the middle of the 18th century the world's population climbed only slowly. And at times of famine and plague, it fell dramatically.

At the beginning of the 15th century, about two million people lived in England and Wales. One hundred years later the figure was about the same. By 1600 it had doubled to just over four million, and by 1700 it had gone up to a little over five million. Then something startling started to happen.

By 1751, the population of England and Wales stood at 5.7 million. Scotland's was about 1.2 million and Ireland's around 2.4 million, for a total of about 9.3 million on the British Isles. Fifty years later, the figure stood at 15.4 million, and over the next 50 years it soared up again, reaching 27.3 million. Villages grew into towns, and towns swelled into cities.

This population increase is even more remarkable considering the large numbers of British emigrating to the American colonies. In 1700, there were 250,000 British people in the colonies. In 1790, the first U.S. census counted 1.5 million citizens with British roots. The relationship between growing population and the Industrial Revolution was a complicated, two-way process. On the one hand, the Revolution allowed some people to earn better wages. This gave them more to spend on food, so they became fitter and had more, healthier children. On the other hand, the soaring population presented business people with new opportunities. More people meant the country needed more of everything—more food, more houses, more pots and pans, more clothes. The demand for clothes, for example, meant that more mills and factories were needed in which to make them. That in turn created more jobs... and in this way the industrial advance continued.

CLASS AND COMMERCE

Europeans in the 18th century were obsessed with class. The British, however, were less obsessed than most. French and Spanish noblemen thought commerce a lower-class activity. British aristocrats were not so fussy. A noble family was proud to make money by improving the agriculture on its estates, then investing this money in a commercial venture. This "culture of profit-making" was another reason why the Industrial Revolution started in Britain, rather than elsewhere in Europe.

The fictional Spanish nobleman Don Quixote was typical of the backward-looking aristocracy of much of Catholic Europe.

Exploring Britain in the late 18th century, Colonel John Byng (1743–1813) did not always like what he saw. A conservative country lover, he did not approve of change, especially when it affected his beloved countryside. After a visit in 1793 to Manchester, for example, he fumed against the growth of towns in the place of green fields.

Husbandman means "farmer."

Sickly traffic refers to the world of business.

But see you not the great increase of Manchester? Yes; I see the hearty **husbandman** suck'd into the gulf of **sickly traffic**; and whilst some towns swell into unnatural numbers, lost is the sturdy yeoman and honest cottager! The business of harvest, formerly the work of three fine weeks, cannot now be finished in six weeks.

Only in 1863 (after censuses in 1851 and 1861) did a government report confirm Byng's anxiety about the movement from country to town.

580 towns were distinguished in 1851, and the population in them and in the surrounding country was nearly equal. But in the subsequent ten years, while the population in the villages and country around increased by half a million... the population in the 580 towns increased by a million and a half... The difference in the rates of increase is due to migration from country to town.

A REVOLUTION IN FARMING

At the time of the British Industrial Revolution, another important change was taking place—the Agricultural Revolution. Scholars do not agree exactly when the Agricultural Revolution happened. Some say it was before the Industrial Revolution; others after it. The most common view is that it was already happening when the Industrial Revolution started, and the two revolutions went on at the same time.

The Agricultural Revolution involved three things: larger farms, an increase in production, and more efficient farming. Farms had been getting bigger for centuries as wealthy farmers bought out the poorer ones. Richer farmers also bought up large areas of open and common land and divided it up into fields enclosed by hedges. This practice became known as enclosure (see box page 15).

The process of enclosure was more or less completed by 1850. In many cases wealthy farmers got permission to enclose by a special Act of Parliament. Larger farms left the countryside peopled by farm owners and landless laborers. As the population was increasing, many landless laborers could not get jobs. They went to look for work in the towns, helping make up the workforce in the new mills and factories.

Food production increased as more land (such as common land) was plowed up. Farming became more scientific, too. New machinery, such as Jethro Tull's seed drill, was used. Pioneers such as Robert Bakewell (improved cattle breeds), Thomas Coke, and Charles "Turnip" Townshend (improved soil and crops) showed what could be done when scientific principles were applied to agriculture.

As farming became more profitable, landowners such as the Duke of Bridgewater had money to spare. Some used it to fund industrial or commercial ventures, such as a canal or mill. In this way the Agricultural Revolution helped feed the Industrial Revolution.

Thomas Coke of Holkham Hall, Norfolk, England, was a pioneer of the Agricultural Revolution. Here he proudly surveys a flock of sheep bred for their (exaggerated!) plumpness.

In the 1820s the journalist and radical politician William Cobbett (1763–1835) made several tours around southern Britain. In 1830 he published his journals as *Rural Rides*. Here are his critical comments about Thanet in East Kent.

ENCLOSURE

Since medieval times, many peasant farmers cultivated small strips of land in large open fields, and kept their animals on common land. But in some parts of the country, land had always been farmed in enclosed fields belonging to an individual farmer. Over the centuries this pattern of farming gradually became more usual. In Kent, for example, open and common land was enclosed as early as the 12th century. Parliament allowed land to be enclosed if the landowners owning more than half the land agreed. This meant that the smaller, poorer families were squeezed out. When commons were enclosed too, thousands of families were forced to become landless laborers, without the right to graze animals or gather firewood from the commons.

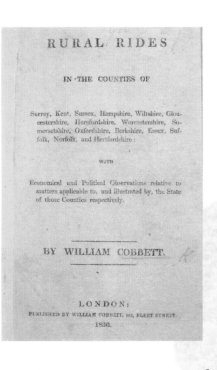

RURAL RIDES

IN THE COUNTIES OF

Surrey, Kent, Sussex, Hampshire, Wiltshire, Gloucestershire, Herefordshire, Worcestershire, Somersetshire, Oxfordshire, Berkshire, Essex, Suffolk, Norfolk, and Hertfordshire:

WITH

Economical and Political Observations relative to matters applicable to, and illustrated by, the State of those Counties respectively.

BY WILLIAM COBBETT.

LONDON:
PUBLISHED BY WILLIAM COBBETT, 183, FLEET STREET.
1830.

William Cobbett was a politician and journalist who campaigned fiercely against the industrialization of English agriculture.

Thanet was once an island.

By the **big bull frog**, Cobbett means "rich farmers."

The laborers' houses, all along through this island, are beggarly in the extreme. The people dirty, poor-looking; ragged but particularly dirty... Invariably have I observed, that the richer the soil, and the more destitute of wood; that is to say, the more purely a corn country, the more miserable the laborers. The cause is this, the great, the big bull frog grasps all. In this beautiful island every inch of land is appropriated by the rich. No hedges, no ditches, no commons, no grassy lanes: a country divided into great farms; a few trees surround the great farmhouse. All the rest is bare of trees; and the wretched laborer has not a stick of wood, and has no place for a pig or cow to graze, or even to lie down upon.

Appropriated by means "taken over by."

MACHINES AND NATURE

Geography and natural resources played a vital part in the British Industrial Revolution. Being an island, Britain had always had a strong maritime tradition, and was ideally placed for trade with both continental Europe and the growing markets in the American colonies and Asia. The many natural harbors around the British coastline also allowed heavy goods to be transported cheaply from one part of the country to the other by sea. By 1790, more than a million tons of coal were being shipped from Tyneside to London each year.

Climate was important, too. One of the major industries of the Industrial Revolution was the manufacture of cotton cloth. It was based in Lancashire, where cotton could be easily worked in the damp atmosphere. Cotton had to be imported from Egypt and colonies in North America and India, but many other raw materials were found in Britain. There were wool for textiles; iron and other metals for engineering; stone and clay for building and pottery; and coal for heating and driving steam engines.

By 1760, several developments had helped industry to expand. Inland transport was improved by the building of "turnpikes"—roads kept in good order by charging travelers a toll. Before turnpikes, most roads were full of ruts and deep potholes. By the 1750s, most of the main roads out of London were turnpikes. Long stretches of river were made navigable by the dredging and the construction of locks. In 1757 the first canal, the Sankey Brook Navigation, was built to take coal from St. Helens to the River Mersey. The famous Bridgewater Canal was started two years later, and by 1830 the country had about 2,980 miles (4,800 km) of canal.

Inventions played their part, too. In the early 18th century Thomas Savery and Thomas Newcomen produced a steam engine for pumping water. In 1709 Abraham Darby discovered how to get pure iron out of iron ore by heating it with coke rather than with charcoal. The textile industry benefited from Lewis Paul's machine for carding (combing) raw cotton and from John Kay's flying shuttle, which speeded up weaving. Although none of these inventions had a major impact at the time, they prepared the way for the changes to come.

A Newcomen steam pump, 1705: Although slow and inefficient, many of these reliable engines were still in use 100 years later.

In his book *A Tour Through the Whole Island of Great Britain* (1724–12) the writer Daniel Defoe (c.1660–1731) frequently came across turnpike roads.

In winter, unmade roads, especially on heavy soil, turned into quagmires in which a person could drown!

Droves means "herds."

Turn-pikes... have been set on the several great roads of England, beginning at London, and proceeding through almost all those dirty deep roads, in the Midland counties especially; at which Turn-pikes all carriages, droves of cattle, and travellers on horseback, are obliged to pay an easy Toll; that is to say, a horse a penny, a coach three pence, a cart four pence... but in no place is it thought a burden... the benefit of a good road abundantly making amends for that little charge...

There were 240 pennies in a pound.

WATERPOWER

Until the 19th century, most machinery was driven by water. Waterwheels produced the power for grinding corn, hammering iron, and making paper, gunpowder, and other products. For many decades waterwheels were also the chief source of energy for the textile industry. Although steam gradually replaced waterpower, some water mills were still operating well into the 20th century.

The entrance to the Tottenham Court Road Turnpike, London, England, in the late 18th century: The collection of tolls allowed many of the country's major roads to be greatly improved.

THE GLOBAL ADVENTURE

For many centuries, British trade centered around the export of wool and woolen cloth and the import of goods such as wine, silks, and spices. In the late 16th century this pattern began to change.

With the opening up of shipping routes to America, Asia, and Africa, British trade expanded enormously. By the mid-18th century, about half of the world's sea trade was carried in British ships. Britain was also building up a network of colonies and trading stations, principally in North America, the Caribbean, and India (see map). These outposts provided cheap raw materials and markets for British goods. By the 1750s, North America was spending £1 million a year on British products.

The pattern of Britain's trade was becoming more complicated,

A British merchant ship sets sail from Liverpool, England, with a cargo of cotton goods for North America.

too. The slave trade is a well-known example (see page 29). Merchants bought captives in Africa and shipped them to the Americas, where they were sold as slaves. The money raised was spent on raw materials, such as sugar and tobacco, which were

BRITAIN'S OVERSEAS COLONIES

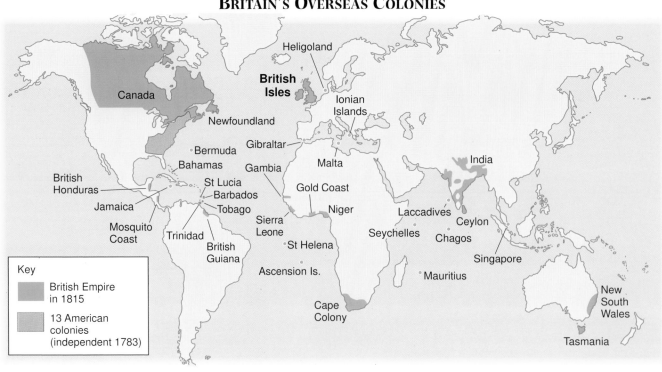

Heligoland

British Isles

Canada

Ionian Islands

Newfoundland

Gibraltar

Bermuda

Bahamas

Gambia

Malta

India

British Honduras

St Lucia

Gold Coast

Barbados

Jamaica

Tobago

Niger

Laccadives

Ceylon

Mosquito Coast

Trinidad

Sierra Leone

Seychelles

Chagos

British Guiana

St Helena

Singapore

Ascension Is.

Mauritius

Cape Colony

New South Wales

Tasmania

Key

British Empire in 1815

13 American colonies (independent 1783)

imported to Europe. Profit from the trade paid for more African slaves, and so the cycle continued.

British trade made the country a center for worldwide commerce, and amassed vast fortunes for successful merchants. In 1700, Britain's imports were worth almost £6 million with exports amounting to almost £6.5 million. By 1800 the figures were £28.3 million for imports and £40.8 million for exports. Over half the profit came from textiles manufactured in Britain. In other words, the Industrial Revolution did not happen in isolation—it was part of a larger, global process.

British merchants and manufacturers also benefited from a secure financial system. Unlike many European governments, the British government (helped by the Bank of England, founded in 1694) kept its debts under control. This gave people confidence in British money. The insurance industry made enterprises less risky. Banks—London had about seventy banks by 1800—lent money at low rates of interest. The establishment in 1773 of the Stock Exchange, where people could buy and sell investments in the government and private companies, also encouraged business investment.

A London coffeehouse in the early 18th century: It was in such a meeting place that the Lloyds insurance business began.

In 1747, Richard Campbell wrote *The London Tradesman*, a guide to trade and commerce in London. In it he gave details of Britain's trade with the Caribbean.

The **Sugar Colonies** was a term for the British islands in the Caribbean, because of the large number of sugar plantations there.

Note that German linen was exported in British ships.

Haberdashery means items such as ribbons.

We export to Jamaica, and the rest of the Sugar Colonies all manner of materials for wearing apparel, household furniture of all sorts, cutlery and haberdashery wares, watches, jewels and toys, East-India goods of all sorts, some French wines, English malt liquor, linen cloths of the growth of Scotland, Ireland and Germany, and our ships generally touch in Ireland and take in provisions, such as beef, pork, and butter. The returns from thence are rums, sugars, cotton, indigo, some fine woods, such as mahogany... and some dying woods, particularly logwood.

This means goods from India and the Far East.

This refers to British imports from the Caribbean.

These are woods that contain a natural dye.

CHAPTER 3

TAKEOFF

SPINNING AND WEAVING

Cloth production had long been an essential part of the British economy (see page 18). Not surprisingly, it was one of the first industries to get caught up in the Industrial Revolution. The amount of cloth produced rose sharply, the industry gradually became more mechanized and moved into factories, and cotton cloth overtook wool as the most profitable British textile.

In 1750 the British textile industry was using about 60 million tons of raw wool and 2.5 million tons of raw cotton a year. The figures for 1800 were about 100 million tons of raw wool and over 50 million tons of raw cotton. Fifty years later they were around 215 million tons of raw wool and 790 million tons of raw cotton! Why did the industry expand in this way?

One reason was simply that the population of Britain had grown, so more clothes, blankets, and other products were required. But as Britain produced far more cloth than it needed, much of it was exported. Why did people buy British cloth rather than make their own? Because of British government policy, those living in the colonies often had little choice but to buy British goods. Others bought British cloth because of its low price.

The use of machinery, based in factories, cut the cost of turning raw wool and cotton into cloth. The two key processes were spinning (twisting loose

Cottage industry in 1791: The development of power spinning made such domestic work uneconomic and forced many laborers' families to look for work in the factories.

fibers into thread) and weaving (making threads into cloth on a loom). Although the flying shuttle (see page 16) and Spinning Jenny (invented by James Hargreaves in 1764) speeded things up, they were originally hand-powered machines. But after Richard Arkwright's construction of a water-driven spinning machine (the water frame, 1769), the cloth industry began slowly to become factory-based.

Further inventions, notably Samuel Crompton's spinning mule (1779) and Edmund Cartwright's power loom (1786), allowed the factory system to produce vast quantities of cloth at great speed. Even so, the change to factory production took many years.

Hargreaves' Spinning Jenny: This model did the work of eight spinning wheels under the supervision of a single operator.

In 1784 Rev. Edmund Cartwright (1743–1823) heard some Manchester businessmen worrying that spinning machines were turning out more thread than the weavers could cope with. Their anxiety started him thinking, and led eventually to the invention of the power loom. This excerpt comes from *The History of Cotton Manufacture in Great Britain, of 1835* by Edward Baines.

Conception means "idea."

Some little time afterwards... recalling this conversation to my mind, it struck me that, as in plain weaving, according to the conception I then had of the business, there could be only three movements which were to follow each other in succession, there would be little difficulty in producing and repeating them. Full of these ideas, I immediately employed a carpenter and smith to carry them into effect. As soon as the machine was finished I got a weaver to put in the warp... To my great delight, a piece of cloth, such as it was, was the product.

The **warp** is the thread that runs the length of the cloth.

RICHARD ARKWRIGHT

Richard Arkwright (1732–92) built some of the first spinning machines and became one of the most successful businessmen of the early Industrial Revolution. He pioneered the factory system, housing his machines in mills powered by horses, water, and finally by steam. Many laborers believed that his machines were putting them out of work, and in 1779 an angry mob burned down his mill in Chorley, Lancashire.

MILL AND FACTORY

The word "mill" was originally used to describe a building that housed machinery. Most villages had their own water mills or windmills for grinding corn; paper and soap were also made in mills. A "factory" (a short form of "manufactory") originally referred to an overseas trading base. In time, however, "factory" came to mean a place where things were manufactured.

Until the Industrial Revolution, most industrial processes, from weaving cloth to making guns, were carried out in workshops or people's homes. From about 1750, some industries (led by textiles and iron) began to switch from small-scale production to large-scale factory (or mill) production. This involved making large quantities of goods in a single place, using power (water or steam) to drive machinery, and having a large, well-organized force of wage-earning workers.

The mills and factories of the early Industrial Revolution were generally big brick buildings, some many stories tall. They were built near a source of power for driving their machinery. At first this meant siting them next to a fast-flowing stream or river, often in beautiful countryside. Later, when steam power became more common, they were built near a coalfield. Coal was needed to fire the engines' boilers.

Owners also liked to position their mills and factories near a source of raw materials. So cotton mills were based in Lancashire, close to the port of Liverpool where cotton arrived from the United States (see pages 32-33). In 1800 there was a cluster of ironworks in a line from Stafford to Coventry, near where iron ore was mined. Because workers needed to live near their place of employment, rows of small houses were put up around the mills, factories, and mines. These houses were often badly built, with poor water supplies and drains (see pages 38-39).

As reserves of coal and other minerals lie mostly in the north and west of Britain, the Industrial Revolution affected that part of the country far more than the south and east.

The Coalbrookdale Ironworks, Shropshire, England, in 1788: Concern about industrial pollution lay a long way in the future.

Dancing lessons in Robert Owen's New Lanark Mills, Scotland, 1825: Owen was one of the few employers who realized that a happy, well-educated workforce was also a more productive one.

NEW LANARK
Welsh businessman Robert Owen (1771–1858) believed everyone would benefit if the fruits of the Industrial Revolution were shared between employers and employees. In 1800 he took over the New Lanark Mills in Scotland and turned them into a model industrial community. His workers were better paid and housed than elsewhere, and were provided with education, childcare, and leisure opportunities.

 Friedrich Engels (see page 9) was very critical of the effects of the factory system on British towns. Here, in *The Condition of the Working Class in England*, he describes industrial Manchester in the 1840s.

...surrounded on four sides by tall factories and high embankments, covered with buildings, stand two groups of about two hundred cottages, built chiefly back to back, in which live about 4,000 human beings... The cottages are old, dirty, and of the smallest sort, the streets uneven, fallen into ruts and in part without drains or pavement; masses of refuse, offal and sickening filth lie among standing pools in all directions; the atmosphere is poisoned by the effluvia from these, and laden and darkened by the smoke of a dozen tall factory chimneys.

Effluvia means poisonous gases.

POWER

The earliest machines were driven by natural forces—animals (including people), wind, and water. As generators of industrial power, all these sources had serious drawbacks. Animals tired and could not drive large machines. Wind and water power, as well as being unreliable, were difficult to convert into rapid motion. Moreover, windmills and water mills could not be moved—so the industrial machinery had to be brought to the power source. The great triumph of the Industrial Revolution was to produce new and mightier sources of power that overcame these difficulties. The first, and in many ways the most important, was steam.

Steam power was already in use by the early 18th century (see page 16). For many years, though, its use was limited to pumping and pressing. This was because there was no way of turning the up-and-down motion of a piston into the circular motion needed to drive the belts and wheels of machinery.

Scottish inventor James Watt (1736–1819) and Birmingham engineer-businessman Matthew Boulton (1728–1809) devised the steam engine that transformed the Industrial Revolution. In 1769 Watt improved the Newcomen engine to make it much cheaper to run. Twelve years later, now in partnership with Boulton, he made a rotative (wheel-turning)

engine. The next year he developed a double-acting engine, in which the steam drove the piston both up and down. This engine produced the powerful rotary motion needed to drive machinery.

Further improvements followed, and by 1800 there were about 2,500 rotative steam engines operating in the country. One-third of them had been made and set up by Boulton and Watt. They were put to all sorts of uses, such as driving bellows and rollers, as well as spinning and

Horse power operating the winding machinery in a French coalmine, 1869: The Industrial Revolution often involved a mixture of old and new technology.

weaving machines. In 1802 Richard Trevithick devised a much more powerful high-pressure engine, and before long the steam engine had taken its most spectacular form—the railway engine.

Even so, the change from water to steam power was slow. Not until the middle of the century did steam become the principal source of power for British industry.

James Watt was the Scottish engineer and inventor responsible for realizing the true potential of steam power.

MATTHEW BOULTON

Matthew Boulton, equally successful as an engineer and businessman, was a typical pioneer of the early Industrial Revolution. He inherited his father's silver-stamping business and, in 1762, re-housed it in the Soho works, Birmingham. Realizing the importance of James Watt's work on steam engines, he backed the idea with his money and commercial experience. He set up the new engines in the Soho works and used them to mint Britain's new copper coinage.

This shows steam engines under construction in the Boulton & Watt workshops at Soho, near Birmingham, England.

Richard Guest was related to pioneer ironmaster Josiah Guest. He was one of the first writers to describe the effect of steam power on the textile industry, in
A Compendious History of the Cotton Manufacture, 1823.

This is a loom driven by a steam engine.

Employers preferred to take on women and young people because they could pay them less.

Guest seems more interested in increased production than the loss of jobs that steam engines brought.

A very good hand weaver, a man 25 or 30 years of age, will weave 2 pieces of... shirting a week, each 24 yards long... A steam-loom weaver, 15 years of age, will in the same time weave 7 similar pieces. A steam-loom factory containing 200 looms, with the assistance of 100 persons under 20 years of age, and of 25 men, will weave 700 pieces per week, of the length and quality before described. To manufacture 100 similar pieces per week by hand, it would be necessary to employ at least 125 looms...

COAL AND IRON

Coal mining was a major British industry long before the Industrial Revolution. In 1700 about 2.5 million tons of coal were extracted from the mines around Newcastle and in South Wales, Lancashire, Shropshire, and southern Scotland. By the end of the century, production had risen to around 11 million tons and was still increasing. Deeper mines were dug, drained by powerful steam-driven pumps.

More coal was produced because more could be sold. As the population rose, there was a greater demand for coal for domestic heating. More important, it was increasingly used by industry. As the country's supplies of wood ran low, coal became the prime fuel for a whole range of other activities, from firing pottery kilns to making soap. The new steam engines also burned coal in their furnaces.

Another big change was pioneered by the Darby family of Coalbrookdale, Shropshire. In the early 18th century, Abraham Darby devised a way of turning iron ore into iron (smelting) by using coke rather than charcoal. This process enabled iron to be produced more cheaply and efficiently. Others (notably Henry Cort) improved the process and, by 1806, only 3 percent of British iron was being made by the charcoal method. As the skill of ironmasters improved, they turned their minds to other ways of using their product. One of the most remarkable of these projects was completed in 1779, when Abraham Darby's grandson (also called Abraham Darby) finished the world's first iron bridge, spanning 98 feet (30 meters) across the River Severn.

In 1720 Britain produced only 25,000 tons of iron and a tiny amount of handmade steel. It imported almost as much from European mines. Over the next century iron imports rose, but domestic production grew much faster. During the early part of the Industrial Revolution, the output of British iron ore mines quadrupled to feed the expanding engineering industry. It was no coincidence that James Watt built his first steam engine at the Carron Ironworks in Scotland. Later, with the railway boom and iron ships, iron output soared to over 6.3 million tons a year.

An early 19th-century English coal mine: Although the mine has a Newcomen pumping engine, much of the hard work is still done by humans and horses.

The iron bridge across the River Severn, England, was painted a year after its completion.

JOHN WILKINSON (1728-1808)

John Wilkinson's ironworks near Wrexham was a major manufacturer of cannons and other weapons. In 1774, Wilkinson invented an extremely accurate machine for boring cannon barrels. He found it also made excellent cylinders for steam engines. Over the next 20 years, Wilkinson provided Boulton and Watt (see page 24) with hundreds of cylinders, and installed one of their steam engines to blow air into his furnaces.

This estimate of the costs involved in making the world's first iron bridge was compiled in about 1777. The estimate came to £3,200 (about $4,800)—a huge sum of money in those days. It was too great an investment for a single businessman, so it was collected from thirteen subscribers (including John Wilkinson and Abraham Darby), all of whom were local ironmasters. They realized that an iron bridge across the River Severn would be a wonderful advertisement for their product.

Abutments are the foundations of the bridge on the riverbanks.

Cast & wrought iron is purified iron heated to a liquid and shaped in a mold.

This estimate for erecting a cast iron bridge (with stone abutments) over the River Severn between Madeley & Broseley. Quantity of cast and wrought iron as near as can be computed amounts to 300 tons... Stone work in abutments... Wrought ashlar... Parapets... Vases and lamp irons... 600 yards of digging and clearing... 111 yards gravelling... Scaffolding to erect the bridge... Making drawings, surveying and other incidents... Making roads [total] £3200.11 [about $4,800]

Wrought ashlar is shaped stone.

Vases and lamp irons are decorative iron vases and posts on which street lamps were hung.

WORKSHOP OF THE WORLD

The Industrial Revolution increased Britain's reliance on trade. More and more raw materials were imported into Britain. Thanks to mechanized industry, they could be processed more efficiently in Britain than in other countries. To complete the cycle, British merchants exported manufactured goods. By the middle of the 19th century, over 90 percent of British imports were raw materials, ranging from cotton to corn. And over 90 percent of the country's exports were manufactured goods.

The volume and value of trade grew at a rate never seen before. By 1825 Britain was spending about $57.5 million a year on imports. One-third of this went to raw materials (mostly cotton) for making textiles. In the same year the value of exports was about $69.5 million. Only 20 years later the value of imports had risen to $121 million, while exports had increased to $189 million!

Britain also had many "invisible earnings." They were called "invisible" because no actual goods changed hands. They included earnings from shipping and insurance, and the profits of money invested abroad, perhaps in a plantation or a mine.

Not surprisingly, Britain boomed. By 1850 one-quarter of the world's trade was passing through British ports. It created more jobs for everyone connected with it, from sailors and dockers to insurers and shipbuilders. The demand for British goods led to more factories, machinery, and houses. At one point 40 percent of the world's manufactured goods were made in Britain, the "workshop of the world."

As we shall see in Chapter Four, this did not automatically mean more money for ordinary working people. Many owners and managers became very rich. But the new wealth filtered down to the pockets of the workers slowly, and often only after bitter protest. The situation was similar in the countries and colonies sending raw materials to Britain. The owners of cotton and sugar plantations, for example, made handsome profits. But those who worked the land, many of whom were slaves, received next to nothing.

Wapping Dock, London, in 1803. Britain's commercial expansion led to a massive growth in dock-building in the capital.

Over the summer of 1851, a Great Exhibition of industry, science, and commerce was held in a gigantic glasshouse (the Crystal Palace) in London's Hyde Park. Over six million visitors came to see its 13,000 exhibits, many of which showed off British industrial and technological prowess. However, the satirical magazine *Punch* often reminded its readers that the country's increasing wealth was far from evenly distributed. In this cartoon it suggested that distressed workers might be put on display alongside the steam engines and looms.

As there were no state pensions and only the well-paid could afford to save for their retirement, many laborers worked until their dying day.

The sewing trade was notoriously poorly paid.

Sweatshop laborers, mostly women, worked long hours at home or in small workshops for pitifully low wages.

For members of the working class, unemployment and sickness often meant starvation.

THE SLAVE TRADE
British ships did not just transport goods. Until 1807, Britain led the world in the trade in slaves from Africa to the Americas. Between 1781 and 1807, British ships carried over one million African captives to slavery. This trade brought huge profits for the merchants, but for the captives themselves it was catastrophic. Many died on board the slave ships before they reached America. Those who survived the crossing were forced to endure lives of extreme poverty and cruelty.

When Daniel Defoe (see page 17) visited Liverpool in the mid 1720s, he made a far-sighted prediction about the expanding port.

An **Exchange** was a business center where cargoes were bought and sold.

The Exchange was not large enough to cope with the huge volume of trade Liverpool was conducting with the Americas.

By the end of the 18th century, Liverpool had indeed become the leading port on Britain's west coast.

The houses here are exceedingly well built, the streets straight, clean and spacious, and they are now well supplied with water. The merchants here have a very pretty Exchange, standing upon 12 free-stone columns, but it begins to be so much too little, that 'tis thought they must remove or enlarge it. This is already the next town to Bristol, and in a little time may probably exceed it, both in commerce, and in numbers of people.

CANALS AND RAILWAYS

Industry needed a reliable and cheap means of transporting raw materials (such as coal and iron) and manufactured goods. There was little point in installing a steam engine, for example, if it could not be supplied with coal at a reasonable price. By the early 19th century, Britain's turnpikes, canals, and coastal shipping provided a good transport network, although each had its drawbacks.

Canal barges and seagoing ships carried heavy loads, but traveled slowly and served only certain areas. Road transport was more flexible, but it, too, was slow and loads were restricted by the power of horses. These problems were solved by the Industrial Revolution's most spectacular development—the construction of a countrywide railway network operated by steam trains.

Railways were not a new idea. In the 18th century, horse-drawn railways were improved by the use of iron rails, wheels, and axles. The next big change came with Watt's invention of a steam engine that could provide rotary power. Even so, it was some time before his idea was applied to transportation.

The first steam locomotives were built in the early 19th century. At first people were suspicious of these noisy, dirty, and dangerous monsters. The turning point came with the opening of the Stockton-Darlington line (1825) and the success of George Stephenson's *Rocket* in locomotive trials held at Rainhill (1829). After the opening of the Liverpool-Manchester line the following year, railway building started in earnest. Within 20 years Britain had some 6,835 miles (11,000 km) of track.

WATERWAYS AND RAILWAYS

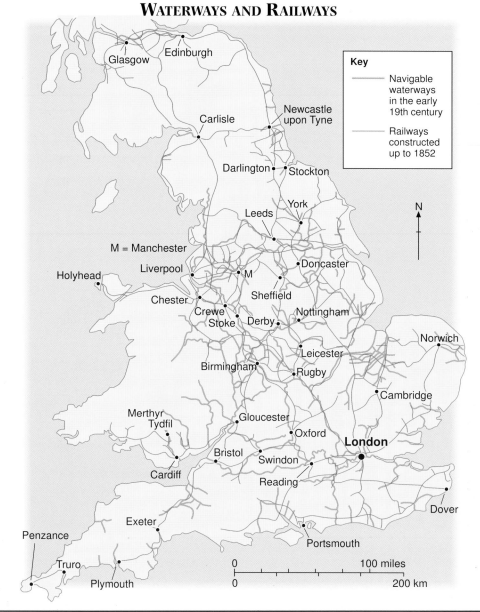

Key

——— Navigable waterways in the early 19th century

——— Railways constructed up to 1852

Glasgow
Edinburgh
Carlisle
Newcastle upon Tyne
Darlington
Stockton
York
Leeds
N
M = Manchester
Liverpool
Holyhead
Doncaster
M
Chester
Sheffield
Crewe
Nottingham
Stoke
Derby
Norwich
Leicester
Birmingham
Rugby
Cambridge
Merthyr Tydfil
Gloucester
Oxford
London
Bristol
Swindon
Cardiff
Reading
Dover
Exeter
Penzance
Portsmouth
Truro
Plymouth

0   100 miles

0   200 km

The Regent's Canal, London, was part of Britain's network of waterways that, for the first time, enabled heavy loads to be carried cheaply and relatively quickly across the country.

The railway boom boosted the iron, steel, and engineering industries; created many new jobs; and made British industry less dependent on textiles. Railways opened up the possibility of much quicker transportation, but they were expensive. For a long time it was cheaper to carry bulky raw materials by canal or sea, and not until the 1850s did railway companies make more money from freight than they did from fare-paying passengers.

George Stephenson's pioneering *Rocket* locomotive was widely admired.

Shortly after she created a sensation with her interpretation of Juliet (in Shakespeare's *Romeo and Juliet*), 21-year-old Frances Kemble became one of the first people to travel on the Liverpool-Manchester Railway. In a letter of August 26, 1830, she describes her ride along the line a few weeks before its official opening.

Unused to steam locomotives, Fanny thought of the machine as a kind of mechanical horse.

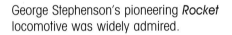

We were introduced to the little engine which was to drag us along the rails... This snorting little animal, which I felt rather inclined to pat, was then harnessed to our carriage, and, Mr. Stephenson having taken me on the bench of the engine with him, we started at about ten miles an hour. The steam-horse being ill-adapted for going up and down hill, the road was kept at a certain level, and appeared sometimes to sink below the surface of the earth... You can't imagine how strange it seemed to be journeying on thus, without any visible cause of progress other than the magical machine...

Frances (Fanny) Kemble

KING COTTON

So far we have talked generally about imports, exports, trade, and industry. Here, we follow one particular crop—an American cotton crop—from its harvest to its export to Britain, its manufacture into cloth, and its re-export back to the United States.

Cotton was originally grown on plantations in the south-eastern United States. By the 1840s, thanks to the invention of the stern-wheel paddleboat (which allowed speedy transport of cotton to the port of New Orleans) and the cotton gin, the crop had spread west to states such as Mississippi and Alabama. Slaves picked the crop by hand. The cotton was cleaned, and gins separated the fibers from the seeds. The cotton fibers were collected in bales ready for shipping to manufacturing areas. Well over half the cotton was loaded into sailing ships bound for Britain.

Liverpool was the principal British cotton port. Bales of cotton were unloaded and transported by canal or rail to the mills. Millworkers fed the raw cotton into water- or steam-powered spinning machines. The thread was then woven on power looms into cloth, which was gathered on huge rolls. It still needed bleaching, dying, or printing before it could be sold as material. These processes were done either in Britain or abroad.

Rolls of cotton cloth, finished or unfinished, were exported around the world. Many went to ports in the northeast of the United States, such as New York and Boston. Here the cloth was cut and sewn into everyday articles such as garments and bedding.

It is not difficult to see that growing cotton in one place, transporting it thousands of miles, turning it into cloth, then transporting it thousands of miles back to its country of origin was a very inefficient process. It was only a matter of time before the United States and other countries adopted British machinery and techniques (see Chapter Five). At this point, the Industrial Revolution was well on the way to becoming a worldwide phenomenon.

Slaves gather cotton in the southern United States in 1860. A high proportion of the crop was exported to Britain for manufacture into cloth.

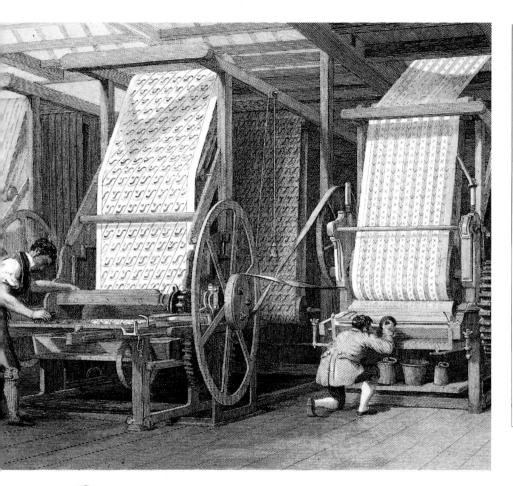

WHITNEY'S COTTON GIN

Two types of cotton grew in the United States, long-staple and short-staple. Long-staple needed a warm, wet climate and good soil. Short-staple grew almost anywhere with a warm climate, but it was difficult to process because the seeds would not separate easily from the cotton fiber. The problem was solved by Eli Whitney, who invented the cotton gin in 1793. As a result, American cotton production soared from 3,000 bales (1790) to 4.8 million bales (1860), three-quarters of the total world output.

Huge rolls of calico (cotton cloth) are printed in a Lancashire factory, 1835.

John Aikin was the son of a teacher and brother of the poet Anna Laetitia Aikin Barbauld. As early as 1795, Aikin was amazed at the extent and prosperity of Robert Peel's cotton mills around Bury in Lancashire. Aikin was a prolific and successful writer, and in *A Description of the Country from Thirty to Forty Miles Round Manchester*, he described how cotton entered the mills as raw material and left them as printed cloth.

The premises occupy a large proportion of ground, and cottages have been built for... the workmen, which form streets, and give the appearance of a village. Ingenious artists are employed in drawing patterns, and cutting and engraving them on wood and copper, and many women and children in mixing and pencilling the colors, etc. The company has several other extensive works in the neighborhood... Some of these are confined to the carding, slubbing, and spinning of cotton; others to washing the cottons with water wheels... Boiling and bleaching the goods are performed at other works. In short, the extensiveness of the whole concern is such as to find constant employ for most of the inhabitants of Bury...

Carding means "combing," and **slubbing** means "preparing for spinning."

Employ means "work."

CHAPTER 4

CONSEQUENCES
MAKING A FORTUNE

Many people argued about the effects of the Industrial Revolution. Opponents pointed to the ugly, overcrowded towns, the ruin of vast areas of countryside, the quest for profit, and the employment of underpaid women and children in dangerous jobs (see page 38). Supporters of the Revolution boasted that it made Britain the most advanced, powerful, and wealthy country in the world. Nothing divided the two sides more than whether or not the Revolution helped ordinary people.

Critics of the new system divided into two groups. One group hankered after a lost past, believing that farmers and agricultural laborers, even when poor, enjoyed better lives than factory workers. The other group accepted the new, socialist thinking. Put very simply, it said that in order to make a profit, business paid its workers the lowest possible wages. As a result, the socialists said, all workers were underpaid, or "exploited."

Modern research confirms that in the long term, the Industrial Revolution made people better off. The British economy grew faster than in any country ever before. It did not, however, make everyone richer, because the new wealth was not evenly distributed. Some groups were desperately poor.

Certain individuals—the owners of land needed for mining or building, for example—became very wealthy. There were plenty of opportunities for successful entrepreneurs, such as the potter Josiah Wedgwood, to make their fortunes, too. In time even the ordinary wage-earning worker gained from the new system. Industrial houses, although small and unsanitary, were more comfortable than most farmworkers' cottages. By the 1850s, standards of living were rising. The average working family spent more on food, heating, clothes, and household goods (such as linen and crockery) than their ancestors had ever done.

The impressive showroom of the Wedgwood and Byerley potteries, St. James's Square, London, was far from the grime of the workshops. Here, the goods were displayed with the utmost elegance.

A contemporary cartoon contrasts the luxury and laziness of the wealthy (above) with the hardships and squalor of the working poor (below).

THE VERY RICH

Many of those who fared the best during the Industrial Revolution contributed least to it. These were the great aristocrats, such as the dukes of Westminster, Portland, Bedford, and Rutland, who inherited vast estates. The value of these lands rose sharply as a result of industrialization and the growth of cities and towns. Some held valuable supplies of minerals; others were sold to builders. When earnings of $450 a year were more than adequate, the Duke of Bedford, owner of Covent Garden, enjoyed an income of over $450,000 a year.

Toward the end of the 18th century, French traveler Barthelemy Faujas de Saint-Fond toured Britain to look into the state of the country's arts, sciences, and natural history. He recorded what he had seen in *A Journey Through England and Scotland* (1774), including one of the first descriptions of Birmingham in the early stages of industrialization.

Curious means "unusual."

Birmingham is one of the most curious towns in all England. If anyone should wish to see in one comprehensive view, the most numerous and varied industries, all combined in contributing to the arts of utility, of pleasure, and of luxury, it is hither that one must come. Here all the resources of industry, supported by the genius of invention, and by mechanical skill of every kind are directed towards the arts, and seem to be linked together to co-operate for their mutual perfection.

The home of "all the resources of industry," Birmingham in 1875

This means creating things.

THE ENVIRONMENT

Wherever the Industrial Revolution took root, it dramatically changed the physical environment. People living at the time were awestruck by the sprawling towns, railway tunnels, embankments, and viaducts, the cavernous warehouses, towering mills, slag heaps as tall as hills, and the infernal glare of the blast furnaces. In the space of only a few generations, huge areas of countryside were transformed from green fields and babbling streams into smoky towns full of roaring activity.

The growth of towns was remarkable. In 1800 only fifteen towns in England and Wales had more than twenty thousand inhabitants. Fifty years later there were sixty-three such towns. London

Contrasting views of industrialization: Gustave Doré's depiction of London slums, 1870 (left) and a painting of a train crossing the Rastrick Viaduct on the London to Brighton railway (below).

expanded to become the largest city in the world. In 1660 it had a population of 450,000; by 1700 this had risen to 575,000, then by 1801 to 980,000. Over the next 40 years the population of London more than doubled to over two million inhabitants.

The balance of the population changed, too. Many ancient southern towns, such as Winchester and Norwich, declined in importance as the population, prosperity, and power moved to the Midlands and the North. The railways not only altered the appearance of the landscape. Small towns where several main lines met, such as Crewe and Rugby, took on a new importance.

The movement of millions of people to London, Liverpool, Leeds, Manchester, Sheffield, Birmingham, and other industrial centers created problems that the authorities had never had to deal with before. How were adequate water supplies to be provided? What was to be done with all the sewage and garbage? Was there any way to control the epidemics of disease such as cholera and typhoid that swept through the overcrowded dwellings? And what about the pollution in the rivers and the smoke-filled air? For years these problems raged out of control, creating poor, industrial areas full of dirt and disease.

CHOLERA

The new industrial towns were breeding grounds for disease of every kind. One of the most vicious was cholera. Spread through drinking water infected with sewage, it killed around 140,000 people in Britain in four epidemics between 1831 and 1866. Although no cure was found, it was prevented by building proper sewers and supplying clean, piped water.

"A Court for King Cholera" from *Punch*, 1852. The spread of the killer disease from the slums to more prosperous districts forced the authorities to take steps to clean up the poorer areas of cities.

Not everyone was impressed by the effects of industrialization. John Byng (see page 13) was appalled when, traveling through North Yorkshire, he came across one of Richard Arkwright's mills near Askrigg.

Profligacy means "wild living."

Prospect means "view."

This means led astray by working and living so close together.

...what has completed the destruction of every rural thought has been the erection of a cotton mill on one side, whereby prospect and quiet are destroyed... the people, indeed, are employed, but they are all abandoned to vice from the throng... At times when people work not in the mill, they issue out to poaching, profligacy and plunder. Sir Richard Arkwright may have introduced much wealth into his family and into the country; but as a tourist, I execrate his schemes, which, having crept into every pastoral vale, have destroyed the course and beauty of nature...

Execrate means "detest."

SLUMS AND SWEAT

In the long term, industrialization brought an overall improvement in living standards. In the short term, however, it caused dreadful suffering. Appalling working conditions and unsanitary housing stand out as two of the most scandalous consequences. Significantly, the conditions revolted many contemporary observers almost as much as they revolt us. Even so, we must be careful not to generalize from the worst examples. While around 80 percent of the population was working class, only a small proportion of mine and factory workers experienced the extreme conditions described here.

Many new mills were airless and incredibly noisy. In some areas, a 14-hour day was common, with only two short breaks, six or even seven days a week. The moving parts on unprotected machinery inflicted the most terrible injuries on its exhausted operators. Apart from days off at Christmas and Easter, holidays were almost unknown.

There are many reports of seven-year-old children being dragged from bed at 5 a.m. and sent off to work in the mills until eight or nine o'clock at night. The conditions in the mines were even worse. Children as young as four sat all day in the dark, hot tunnels, operating air vents. By the age of eight or nine, boys and girls might move on to "hurrying"—hauling small coal trucks down tiny shafts by means of a chain attached to their waist. Because of the heat, they often worked naked.

Conditions at home were little better. A single family of eight might share one damp room, with a single bed, in a bleak courtyard. The toilet was a bucket or a hole in the ground; it and the water pump were shared with many others. Poor children had no schooling whatsoever. Even more shocking to their educated contemporaries, many of them never went to church. Not surprisingly, those who survived in this cruel and disease-ridden world grew up to be both sickly and ignorant.

Children had always been used as a plentiful source of cheap labor, but rarely in conditions as inhuman as those created by rapid industrialization.

This example of a mill supervisor's cruelty was reported to Parliament in 1832.

...there was a young woman who had been kept seven months in the gaol [jail] in Dundee for deserting this mill; and she was brought back... to make up for the lost time and the expenses incurred. One day I was alarmed by her cries. She was lying on the floor, and the master had her by the hair of her head, and was kicking her in the face till the blood was running down.

Factory cruelty: This is an illustration from the title page of Richard Cobden's campaigning publication *The White Slaves of England,* 1853.

Friedrich Engels (see page 9) reported the dreadful overcrowding in the parish of Bethnal Green, London, in the early 1840s.

It contains 1,400 houses, inhabited by 2,795 families, or about 12,000 persons. The population upon which this large population dwells, is less than 400 yards (1,200 feet) square, and in this overcrowding it is nothing unusual to find a man, his wife, four or five children, and, sometimes, both grandparents, all in one single room of ten to twelve square feet, where they eat, sleep and work.

This picture of a slum garret in London's Bethnal Green, from the *Illustrated London News* of 1843, pricked the conscience of the nation and fed the campaign for reform.

THE LABOUR MOVEMENT

In the past, with the exception of London, ordinary working people had been scattered throughout the land, working on farms and in small, local businesses. There was little sense of these people belonging to a group with common needs. Only occasionally were their voices heard on political matters, and then only at times of great upheaval, such as the Peasants' Revolt (1381) or the Civil Wars (1642–48).

The Industrial Revolution changed this, turning working people into an important political force. Industrialization brought them together in large numbers in workplaces and towns. Here, with the help of improved communications, they could exchange ideas. A feeling of working-class comradeship developed, which blossomed into the Labour movement.

The Labour movement gave power to the working classes. In its crudest form, it used the power of the mob, such as the machine-smashing Luddites (see box page 41). In the 1830s and '40s the working-class Chartist movement campaigned for political equality and social justice, demanding (unsuccessfully) that Parliament accept their charter of reforms. Workers also formed friendly and cooperative societies, and many other mutual support groups. The most effective were "combinations," or trade unions. Overcoming all kinds of legal difficulties, unions eventually won the right to withdraw their labor ("strike") and went on to form their own political party, the Labour Party.

Industrialization probably helped improve the status of

The Peterloo Massacre: In August 1819, a large but peaceful crowd assembled to hear speeches on parliamentary reform in St. Peter's Fields, Manchester. When the crowd was attacked by incompetent soldiers, eleven people were killed and about 400 wounded. The ironic name "massacre" echoed Britain's recent victory over Napoleon at Waterloo.

women, too. The millions of new jobs in factories, mills, stores and offices gave many women an opportunity to earn their own money for the first time. Money in the purse was the first step toward independence. Women were nearly always paid less than men, however, and it took years to remove the legal barriers of gender discrimination.

THE LUDDITES

In 1811–12, skilled workers from Nottinghamshire, Yorkshire, and Lancashire rioted and smashed machinery that was putting them out of work. They took their name from a young man named Ned Ludd, who soon became a mythological Robin Hood-type figure known as King Ludd. The movement fizzled out after the execution of seventeen Luddites in York in 1813.

This shows Luddite machine-wreckers at work in 1812.

This is a depiction from *Punch* of the presentation of the third People's Charter for political reform to Prime Minister Russell, 1848.

The People's Charter, presented to Parliament in 1842, was a fascinating example of working people's complaints about the way the country was governed. Although it was rejected (leading to riots and strikes), the fact that the Charter was supposedly signed by over three million people made the ruling classes take notice of working-class demands. Here are two of the Charter's many clauses:

This refers to the House of Commons. Notice that the Charter uses traditional, very respectful language.

This refers to Queen Victoria.

About $250.

Less than $.02.

...your honorable House has not been elected by the people; ...the population of Great Britain and Ireland is at the present time about twenty-six millions of persons; and... yet, out of this number, little more than nine hundred thousand have been permitted to vote... your petitioners, with all due respect and loyalty, would compare the daily income of the Sovereign Majesty with that of the thousands of the working men of this nation; and whilst your petitioners have learned that Her Majesty receives daily for her private use the sum of £164. 17s 10d., they have also ascertained that many thousands of the families of the laborers are only in receipt of 3d. per head per day.

REFORM

Fears and hopes: French revolutionaries resort to violence in Paris, 1789 (above) and (below) Manchester Town Hall, a proud symbol of the triumph of peaceful civic progress.

The Industrial Revolution forced governments to rethink their role. Previously, the attitude of most Western governments toward social matters had been what is often described as "laissez-faire." This meant that it was up to workers and employers to sort out matters such as wages and working conditions between themselves. But the scandals of slums, child labor, long hours, and the inhumane treatment of employees showed that laissez-faire could not work in an industrial society.

So, out of the horrors of the mines and mill towns was born the modern idea of government as a sort of watchdog or protector. Attitudes changed partly out of a genuine wish to improve the lot of the workers and partly out of a fear that unless the government did something, the workers would take matters into their own hands and rebel —as the French had in 1789.

The result was a long campaign of reform. It ranged from relatively simple measures, such as Britain's 1819 Factory Act, which banned children under nine years of age from working in cotton mills, to the state providing unemployment pay, pensions, education, and even medical care. Local governments were given new powers to clear slums, pave streets, and install sewers, fresh water, and street lighting. To pay for these changes and the army of inspectors and other officials needed to enforce them, governments increased taxes considerably.

Many governments also tried to stop businesses from becoming too powerful. The most extreme solution to this and other problems of industrialization was communism. In a communist country, the government took over all land and businesses and ran them for the benefit of everyone. But communist governments were often too powerful and easily corrupted, and lack of competition made their businesses inefficient. Several European democracies experimented with a form of government known as socialism. In these countries, the government took over key industries, such as the railways, but left smaller ones in private hands.

KARL MARX

German thinker Karl Marx was the founder of communism. He said that the Industrial Revolution would lead to political revolutions, when the workers would rise up and take over government and businesses and set up communist states. One day, he believed, these states would disappear, to be replaced by a near-perfect, classless world in which all wealth would be shared equally. Although these ideas proved impractical, for many people in the working classes they helped to explain the present and give hope for the future.

This is Karl Marx at his desk in London, 1852. Marx and Friedrich Engels (see page 9) worked together to write the *Communist Manifesto* (1848), which set out the principles of communism.

The 1839 Report of the British Poor Law Commissioners outlined the effects of disease in city slums and suggested that it was the government's duty to do something about the dreadful conditions—and not simply to help the poor.

This refers to the poor.

The **causes** were bad housing and lack of sanitation.

This refers to people who are not working class.

No returns can show the amount of suffering which they have had to endure from causes of this kind during the last year; but the present returns indicate some of the final results of that suffering; they show that out of 77,000 persons 14,000 have been attacked with fever... and that out of the 14,000 attacked nearly 1,300 have died. The public, meantime, have suffered to a far greater extent than they are aware of, from this appalling amount of wretchedness, sickness and mortality. Independently of the large amount of money which they have had to pay in the support of the sick... they have suffered more seriously from the spread of fever to their own habitations and families. It is notorious that this disease... has found its way even into the dwellings of the rich, where it has proved extremely mortal.

TRADE AND IMPERIALISM

Shipbuilders began to make use of both iron and steam in the 19th century. The first steam ships, built in Britain and the United States, were uneconomic and too unreliable for oceangoing service. These problems were overcome when, in 1838, the *Sirius* made the first all-steam transatlantic crossing. After this, steam power gradually came to dominate, although cargo-carrying sailing ships remained in use well into the 20th century.

The man who did most to promote iron-built ships was Isambard Kingdom Brunel. In 1843 he launched the first iron-hulled, oceangoing ship, the *Great Britain*. The change to metal-hulled, steam-driven vessels gave a tremendous boost to British industry. By the end of the century more than half of the world's ships were built in Britain.

At the same time, Britain began to face increasingly fierce competition from more recently industrialized nations, notably the United States and Germany. World trade, carried in bigger, faster, and more reliable ships, was growing. Companies tried to outdo each other in finding new sources of raw materials and new markets for their goods.

This quest for fresh markets led to a new wave of Western imperialism—the acquisition of overseas empires. The West used its technological superiority to open up trade with China on very favorable terms. In 1847, for example, the British used their naval strength to force the Chinese to hand over Hong Kong and accept the trade in opium, from which British merchants made vast sums of money. Later, European countries took control of large areas of Indochina and almost the whole of the African continent.

The imperial powers quickly brought new colonies into their commercial network, digging mines and building railways and factories. By the early 20th century the effects of industrialization were being felt all around the globe.

The launch of the *Great Britain* at Bristol, 1843: The largest vessel of its day, the all-iron ship was the first to be screw (propeller) driven.

Isambard Kingdom Brunel (1806–59) stands in front of the anchor chains of the *Great Eastern*.

PROTECTION AND FREE TRADE

Britain protected its own goods and industries by charging duties (taxes) on goods coming from other countries. This practice is called protectionism. However, since British manufacturers relied on raw materials from abroad, politicians and business people gradually came around to the idea of "free trade"—the abolition of all duties. The policy was adopted by the mid-19th century, allowing merchants to buy materials where they were cheapest and sell goods where they could get the best price. But by the end of the century, fierce competition abroad was starting to undermine the policy.

For a long time the issue of free trade centered around the Corn Laws—laws that assisted British farmers by not allowing cheap foreign corn into the country. Following the abolition of the Corn Laws in 1846, there was strong pressure to extend free trade into all other areas. This resolution was accepted by the House of Commons in November 1852.

A cartoon drawing portrays Sir Robert Peel, the prime minister responsible for repealing Britain's Corn Laws and so advancing the policy of free trade.

This refers to the House of Commons.

Industrious means "working."

This means free trade.

Supporters of free trade always took the stance that it helped ordinary people, tactfully not mentioning that it helped merchants and business people even more.

That it is the opinion of this House, that the improved condition of the country, and especially of the Industrious Classes, is mainly the result of recent legislation, which has established the principle of unrestricted competition, has abolished taxes imposed for the purposes of protection, and has thereby diminished the cost and increased the abundance of the principle articles of the food of the people... this policy [should be] firmly maintained and prudently extended... and will thereby most surely promote the welfare and contentment of the people.

This means the repeal of the Corn Laws.

CHAPTER 5

THE REVOLUTION SPREADS

EXPANSION

The Industrial Revolution spread first from Britain into those parts of northwest Europe (France, Belgium, and Prussia) where the conditions were right for industrial development. This meant accessible coal and iron, educated engineers and entrepreneurs, and plenty of labor. When European governments saw the wealth and power that industrialization brought, they were eager to help businesses develop those advantages.

At first European industrialization followed the British pattern, with many of the same results and problems. Pioneers benefited from British experience, importing ideas, techniques, and machinery (such as George Stephenson's railway engines). British workers, financiers, and entrepreneurs moved abroad, too. One of the main differences between British and European development was that whereas British enterprises raised their own money, European governments often provided the funds to start up new businesses. The Belgian railway network, for example, was built and run by the state. In contrast, British railways were built and operated by private companies.

Before long, continental Europe had inventors and business tycoons to rival any in Britain. The power loom, invented by the Frenchman Joseph Jacquard, revolutionized patterned weaving. The steelworks of Alfred Krupp of Essen, Germany, led the world in the manufacture of armaments.

The Jacquard loom was designed by the French silk weaver Joseph Marie Jacquard in the early 19th century. The weaving pattern program was set out on a card with holes punched in it, an idea that was later used in early computers.

In about 1870, a second Industrial Revolution began. Industry widened its production from iron, coal, and textiles to include steel, electricity, chemicals, and, eventually, oil and the internal combustion engine.

Industrialization also spread farther afield, into Sweden, Russia, and Italy, across the Atlantic to the eastern United States, and to Japan. By 1900 Britain had lost its industrial supremacy to Germany and, more significantly, the United States. The "American Century" was about to begin.

ALFRED KRUPP (1812–87)

Alfred Krupp was born in Essen, in what was to become the Ruhr industrial heartland of Germany. In 1837, Krupp began manufacturing arms in the small forge he had inherited from his father. He was one of the first to realize the importance of the new process for manufacturing steel (forcing air through molten iron to remove impurities) invented by the British scientist Sir Henry Bessemer (1855). By the time of his death, Krupp's huge business empire included mines and docks as well as steelworks.

Alfred Krupp was Europe's leading steelmaker.

 This British cartoon of 1910 reflects the nation's anxiety at the prospect of losing its position as the world's leading trading nation. More modern machinery sometimes gave the countries that industrialized later a competitive edge over British manufacturers.

John Bull, the figure traditionally used to represent Britain, was an 18th-century farmer type, not an industrialist.

GERMANY AND RUSSIA

The British government may have helped create the conditions for an Industrial Revolution, but it did little to bring it about. In contrast, the German and Russian governments noted the benefits of industrialization and actively encouraged it, mainly by providing capital (money).

Although by 1809 parts of the industrial Ruhr Valley in Westphalia were being called a "miniature England," early German industrialization was fairly disorganized and scattered. The 1834 Zollverein (Customs Union) removed tariffs on trade between individual German states, and the construction of

railways boosted commerce. Even so, the most dramatic growth followed the unification of the German states into a single country in 1871.

In partnership with the government, which made reasonable loans available from a national bank, German industry began to expand. The growth of older industries (iron, coal, textiles) was matched by newer ones, such as electricity and the internal combustion engine. By 1914 steel output in Germany was double that in Britain. German ingenuity and technology backed the development of the generator (Ernst Siemens), electric traction,

and the automobile (Karl Benz). German shipyards built many of the world's finest ocean liners and warships.

In 1860 Russia was a land of peasant farmers and small family workshops. However, it developed even more quickly than Germany. The key figure was Finance Minister (and later Prime Minister) Count S. I. Witte, who protected Russian industry with tariffs and raised huge foreign loans, mostly from France. Under his guidance, Russian industry grew rapidly in the 1890s.

By 1914 Russia's economy was one of the top five in the world. The country produced half

INDUSTRY IN EUROPE

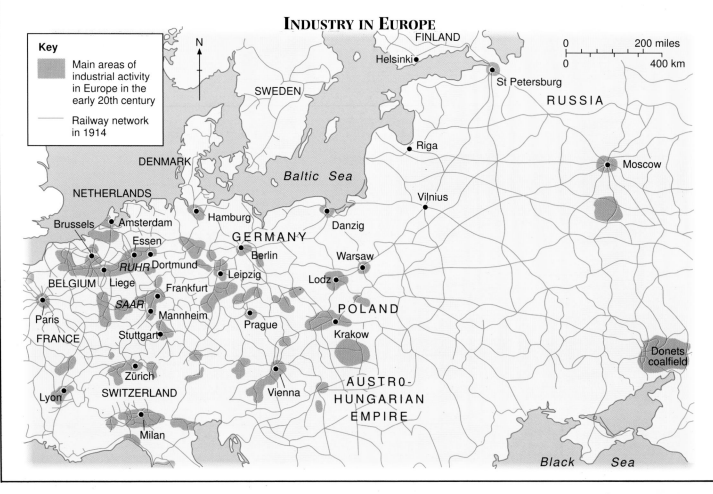

Key

Main areas of industrial activity in Europe in the early 20th century

Railway network in 1914

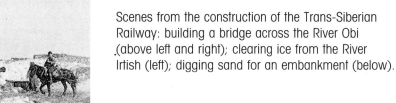

Scenes from the construction of the Trans-Siberian Railway: building a bridge across the River Obi (above left and right); clearing ice from the River Irtish (left); digging sand for an embankment (below).

of the world's crude oil. Its state-funded railway-building program, including the famous 4,387-mile (7,060-kilometer) Trans-Siberian line between Moscow and Vladivostok, was second only to that of the United States. But the price of this dash for growth was high: In 1917 a large and angry industrial working class overthrew the government that had brought it into being.

One feature of Russia's industrialization was the housing of industrial workers in barracks rather than houses. The condition of these barracks was often appalling, as an inspector of the Bryansk metallurgical factory reported in 1892.

It is no exaggeration to say that these dwellings can be compared with the quarters of domestic animals: their unwashed and filthy condition is unlike anything found in a human living-place. Even in summer, when the windows and doors are left open, the air is stifling; slime and mold sticks to the walls and bunk-beds, and the floors are invisible beneath a carpet of filth.

THE RUSSIAN REVOLUTIONS

In the early years of the 20th century, Russia experienced three revolutions. The first (1905) forced the czar (emperor) to accept a *duma* (parliament). The second (February 1917) set up a Western-style government, while the third revolution (October 1917) brought the Communists to power. The three revolutions were brought about by the new power of the industrial working class, produced by the country's rapid industrialization.

THE INDUSTRIALIZATION OF THE UNITED STATES

The foundations of the Industrial Revolution in the United States were laid before the outbreak of the Civil War (1861). Although most Americans lived in the countryside, by the middle of the century the value of manufacturing output had overtaken agriculture. About 31,000 miles (50,000 km) of railroad track had been laid. In parts of the Northeast, a factory system was thriving. The most famous example was the cotton mills of Lowell, Massachusetts. This first American "mill town" was built by Francis Cabot Lowell, who introduced the power loom and the integrated factory to American manufacturing. By 1850, the city was described by some European visitors as one of the wonders of the world. Huge five-story brick mills lined the banks of the Merrimack River. The flow of water powered 320,000 spindles and 10,000 looms. The factory employed over 10,000 workers.

Industrialization on this scale in the United States was an unsurprising development, for the country had ample supplies of virtually every known natural resource: minerals such as iron, coal, oil, and lead; plentiful food and timber; and navigable waterways, natural harbors, and fast-flowing rivers.

After the end of the Civil War in 1865, the United States entered a period of extraordinary growth driven by the railroad industry. By 1890, railroad companies had built 165,300 miles (266,000 km) of track and employed 36,000 people. They allowed a national economy to develop by enabling products to

Westward the Course of Empire Takes Its Way: This romantic painting of an early railroad by the American artist F. E. Palmer reflects the energy and pride of American industrialization.

be transported swiftly anywhere in the country. Moreover, railroad construction provided work for many related industries, such as iron, steel, engineering, building, quarrying, and lumbering.

A few statistics give some idea of the scale of the revolution. In 50 years (1850–1900) U.S. exports rose from $152 million to $1.9 billion. By 1900, the United States produced more steel than Britain and Germany combined. Coal output soared from 20.5 million tons in 1870 to 212.3 million tons in 1900. U.S. inventors, who registered 1.5 million new inventions between 1860 and 1890, dreamed up the lightbulb, typewriter, telephone, and countless other devices we now take for granted.

THOMAS EDISON (1847–1931)

Although he received little formal education, Thomas Edison became the wizard of American invention. During his lifetime he took out over one thousand patents for a wide range of gadgets and devices, including the electric storage battery, the electric valve, the movie camera, the gramophone, and an improved microphone. His most famous invention, however, was probably one of the simplest—the electric lightbulb.

Thomas Edison with his gramophone.

In America, far more than in Britain, the Industrial Revolution brought hope and opportunity. Americans felt that almost anyone who worked hard and had a bit of luck could become a millionaire. For the ambitious, the advice of steel millionaire Andrew Carnegie in *The Road to Business Success* (1885) was almost compulsory reading.

Andrew Carnegie was one of the many multimillionaires produced by the industrialization of America.

Assuming that you have obtained employment and are fairly started, my advice to you is "aim high." I would not give a fig for the young man who does not already see himself the partner or the head of an important firm... Say to yourself, "My place is at the top." Be king in your dreams ... And here is the prime condition of success, the great secret: concentrate your energy, thought, and capital exclusively upon the business in which you are engaged. Having begun in one line, resolve to fight it out on that line, to lead in it, adopt every improvement, have the best machinery, and know the most about it.

THE AMERICAN WAY

In 1913, John D. Rockefeller (above) set up the Rockefeller Foundation "to promote the well-being of mankind." Below, boys are shown at work in a South Carolina cotton mill, 1900.

America faced the same problems as other 19th-century industrialized countries. Workers, many of them new arrivals from Europe, endured shameful conditions in sprawling industrial cities. In response, a labor movement grew up, leading to the familiar pattern of strikes and even violence. At the other extreme, a number of men (sometimes known as robber barons) became fantastically wealthy. Unlike many of their British counterparts, most came from humble origins. John D. Rockefeller, for example, rose from bookkeeper to billionaire oil magnate through a combination of hard work and good fortune.

Industrialization played a key role in welding the United States together. The country had begun when thirteen separate and very different states came together under an overall (federal) government. Each state kept its own laws, administration, and customs. Although the Civil War confirmed, by force, that states could not leave the Union, it took the Industrial Revolution to bind them into a modern country.

Industrialization and the revolution in communications (railways, the telegraph, and the telephone) turned the country into a single, gigantic marketplace. For example, iron ore mined near Lake Superior could be processed in Ohio into plows, which were then transported to the farmers of

California. By the turn of the century, hundreds of thousands of similar operations linked every town, city, and state in a vast web of commerce.

The federal government assisted industry through such measures as grants of land and tariffs on foreign goods. But following the principle "Government that governs least governs best," it left the regulation of commerce and industry largely to the states and businesses themselves. Later, however, starting with the Interstate Commerce Act (1887), it began to oversee and control businesses. In this way the Industrial Revolution changed not only the way Americans lived and worked, but even the way they were governed.

 The American Industrial Revolution, like the British, began in the spirit of laissez-faire (see page 42). Employers such as Henry V. Rothschild believed that no government had a right to interfere in the contract between him and his employees. He made his position quite clear before a House of Representatives committee in 1879.

UNION PACIFIC RAILROAD COMPANY

The Union Pacific Railroad was the first to cross the North American continent. Construction began in 1862, backed by massive federal loans and grants of land, and was completed in 1869 when it met the Central Pacific line from San Francisco at Promontory Point, Utah. The line was vital to the opening up of California, Colorado, Nebraska, and Wyoming to immigrants and commercial enterprises of every kind.

The line is complete: Promontory Point, 1869.

The **legislature** is the law-making body—Congress or a state legislature.

This means those with "capital"—the employers and factory owners.

I say the legislature has no right to encroach upon me as to whether I shall employ men eight hours, or ten, or fifteen hours. It is a matter of mutual agreement, and the legislature has no right, according to the principles of the Declaration of Independence, to impose upon me what hours of labor I shall have between myself and my employees... Political economy teaches us that the laborers and the capitalists are two different forms of society... The laborer should do as good as he can for himself, and the capitalist should do as good as he can for himself; it is a matter between the laborer and the capitalist.

This is the document by which the American colonies declared themselves independent from Britain, in 1776.

This refers to the social sciences.

JAPAN'S CULTURAL BORROWING

Emperor Mutsuhito: His reign marked the beginning of Japan's remarkable industrialization.

East meets West: The Japanese warship *Yashima* visits Newcastle, England, in 1902. The Anglo-Japanese alliance of that year reflected Japan's newfound status as a world power.

In 1858, Western imperialist powers, including the United States, forced Japan to accept "unequal treaties," which gave them very favorable trading rights. Leading Japanese politicians and thinkers, fearing their country might become another Western colony, overthrew the government (1868) and under the young Emperor Mutsuhito set about turning Japan into a modern, industrialized state.

The Japanese followed a policy of "cultural borrowing." They accepted that many Western ways—in government as well as industry and technology—were more advanced than their own, and began copying them. From 1871–73, a group of forty Japanese politicians and leaders toured Europe and the United States. This group was called the Iwakura Mission. The report

of the mission, covering every aspect of life from mining to medicine, inspired the world's first deliberate industrialization.

The government led the way. It used one-third of the money it collected in taxes to develop commerce and industry, founding the Bank of Japan (1877) and building model steel and textile factories. Japanese students were sent abroad to study foreign ways, and domestic education was modernized and expanded. By the end of the century about 90 percent of Japanese children went to school, a figure that was bettered by only a handful of Western countries such as Britain and Germany.

All aspects of economic life benefited from the government's drive to modernize the country. The traditional silk industry moved into steam-powered factories. Agricultural output tripled between 1870 and 1900. This meant not only more food, but also more tax for the government to invest in industry. Coal output rose from under one million tons before 1885 to 21 million tons in 1914. In 1869 the first Japanese-built modern ship crossed the Pacific. Only 45 years later Japan had 1.4 million tons of merchant shipping and a navy that ranked among the best in the world.

The Japanese achievement was remarkable. In 50 years it transformed itself into a powerful industrialized state, the first in Asia capable of holding its own among the world's most powerful nations. By the time of World War I (1914–18), the Industrial Revolution was no longer simply a Western phenomenon.

THE IWAKURA MISSION

Named after its leader, Iwakura Tomomi, the Iwakura Mission was divided into three sections: political, economic, and educational. The members of the mission spent seven months in the United States, four in Britain, and further time in other European countries. The information gathered by the economic section from its visits to banks, mines, and factories was later published and became a blueprint for Japan's Western-style modernization.

The Iwakura Mission leaves for the United States, in 1871.

From the start of their modernization, the Japanese made it quite clear that their copying of Western ways was purely for practical purposes: Unless the country industrialized, it would not be strong enough to preserve its independence. In 1889 Kuga Katsunan explained this position in the newspaper *Nihon*.

We recognize the excellence of Western civilization. We value the Western theories of rights, liberty and equality; we respect Western philosophy and morals... Above all, we esteem Western science, economics, and industry. These, however, ought not to be adopted simply because they are Western; they ought to be adopted only if they can contribute to Japan's welfare.

AN INDUSTRIAL WORLD

Over the course of the 20th century, industrialization continued to spread around the world. Because it was originally a Western development, growing out of an American-European society and culture, it tended to take root most readily in parts of the world where Western influence was strongest. These included South America and Britain's former colonies, such as Canada, Australia, and New Zealand.

In most of Africa and Asia (the obvious exceptions being South Africa and Japan), industry tended to develop in pockets, such as the areas around the ports of Calcutta and Shanghai, which had traditions of contact with the rest of the world. Apart from the arrival of the railways, until the middle of the century many areas remained largely untouched by industrial development.

In the end, though, the march of industry proved irresistible. By the 1990s it had penetrated every corner of the globe. As they had in Britain 200 years previously, people traded the countryside for crowded cities. They no longer lived off the land but sought jobs with regular hours and pay. Instead of making the things they needed, or buying them from a local craftworker, they bought factory-made products in stores.

All this, together with the revolution in transport and communication, stemmed directly from the Industrial Revolution. It has lifted billions out of poverty, widened the gap between the rich nations and the poor, and brought terrible destruction on the environment. In short, the Industrial Revolution triggered the biggest change in human life since the introduction of farming, around 10,000 B.C. Moreover, it is one we are still learning to come to terms with.

"Technological Innovation Causes New Red Flowers to Bloom." This Chinese propaganda poster from the late 1960s reinforced the message that to compete in the modern world, China had to become an industrial nation.

This is a modern cotton mill in Ahmedaba, India, a city known locally as "the Manchester of the East."

GLOBAL WARMING

The energy for the Industrial Revolution came from burning fossil fuels—coal and oil. These fuels release gases, particularly carbon dioxide, into the atmosphere. In 1967, scientists suggested that these gases might build up in the atmosphere and act like the glass of a greenhouse, keeping in the sun's heat. By the 1990s, temperatures on Earth were definitely rising. Might this be the Industrial Revolution's most catastrophic legacy?

Smog hangs over Mexico City.

 By the middle of the 20th century, just about every country in the world wished to be industrialized. It was not just a matter of wealth, but of power. In 1945, Soviet dictator Joseph Stalin warned his people (in·*The Problems of Leninism*) to accept either swift industrialization —or humiliation.

To slacken the tempo [of industrial advance] would mean falling behind. And those who fall behind get beaten... It is the jungle law of capitalism. You are backward, you are weak—therefore you are wrong; hence you can be beaten and enslaved. You are mighty—therefore you are right; hence we must be wary of you... That is why we must no longer lag behind... We are fifty or a hundred years behind the advanced countries. We must make good this distance in ten years. Either we do it, or they crush us.

GLOSSARY

aristocrat Someone of noble birth; for example, a prince or princess, duke or duchess.

barracks Accommodation for soldiers or workers.

capital Surplus money that can be invested in a business. A capitalist is someone who has money to invest, or who earns his or her living by investment rather than work. Capitalism is the economic system based on investment and profit, such as that in Britain and the United States at the time of the Industrial Revolution.

census A population count.

Chartism The British working-class movement that demanded political reforms, such as the right to vote and annual elections. The Chartists put forward their ideas in petitions called charters, which were presented to Parliament in 1839 and 1842.

cholera A disease of the intestine caused by drinking water infected by sewage. In the 19th century it was frequently fatal.

coalition A government made up of members of two or more parties.

coke Coal that has been heated in the absence of air. During the Industrial Revolution, coke replaced charcoal as the heating agent used to separate iron from iron ore.

colony An overseas territory belonging to the empire of an imperialist power.

combination An early word for a trade union.

commerce All kinds of business, trade, buying, and selling.

communism A political and economic philosophy, most passionately put forward by Karl Marx. It states that all property and wealth should be owned by the state and shared equally among all citizens. The principles of communism were set out by Karl Marx and Friedrich Engels in the *Communist Manifesto* (1848).

crude oil Oil that has not been refined into fuel oil, lubricants, or other products.

enclosure The act of fencing in common land or large fields by one farmer that up to that point had been worked by several farmers.

entrepreneur A business person who takes risks and tries new commercial enterprises.

export To sell raw materials or goods from one country to another. The sum of such materials or goods is known as a country's exports.

factory system Large-scale manufacture in one place, using machinery and a wage-earning labor force.

federal In the United States, relating to the national government in Washington, D.C., rather than the governments of the individual states. For example, the federal government is responsible for foreign policy and regulating trade between the states.

free trade The absence of tariffs on international commerce.

freight Goods carried by land, sea, or air from one place to another.

generator A machine for generating electricity.

Glorious Revolution The events of 1688 in Britain when James II was replaced on the throne by his daughter, Mary, and her husband, William of Orange.

immigrant Someone who enters a country to live and work there.

imperialist A person or country that seeks to build up an empire by taking over other lands as colonies.

import To bring raw materials or goods into a country from abroad. The sum of such materials or goods is known as a country's imports.

interest rate The amount charged to borrow money.

invest To put money into a commercial enterprise.

Jacobites Supporters of the Catholic King James II and his successors. There were Jacobite rebellions in 1715 and 1745.

laissez-faire The philosophy, widely followed in the early years of the Industrial Revolution, that it is not the government's job to interfere in commercial activity.

legislation Laws.

loom A weaving machine.

Luddites Early 19th-century handcraft workers who attacked factories and broke machinery because they feared industrialization was depriving them of their livelihood.

market The place where goods are sold. It may mean a local market or, in a broader sense, all areas where goods are sold. In the early 19th century, for example, Lancashire was the principal market for American cotton.

mill The original word for a place, such as a water mill, where machinery was used in manufacture.

patent The registration of a new design or invention so that it cannot be copied by someone else without permission.

protectionism Keeping out goods made in other countries by charging high tariffs.

shares A common way of investing money in a commercial enterprise. In return for buying a share in a company, the shareholder receives a proportion (the dividend) of the company's profit —if it makes any.

socialism A philosophy derived from communism. Socialists believe governments should control industry and commerce, ensuring that their benefits are shared fairly among all citizens.

Steel pure iron to which a little carbon has been added to make it tougher and less brittle.

Strike when workers withdraw their labor (refuse to work), bringing the business they work in to a halt. Strikes are usually called to improve pay and conditions.

tariff A tax or "duty" raised on goods entering a country.

textiles All woven materials, such as cotton, wool, and linen.

trade Buying and selling between one country and another. The "balance of trade" is the difference between the amount spent on imports and that earned from exports.

trade union A society of workers, usually from the same type of employment, formed to protect and help those workers.

turnpike A road for which maintenance is paid by charging users a toll.

typhoid A highly infectious disease of the intestine, usually caught through drinking contaminated water. It was widespread among the expanding towns of the early Industrial Revolution.

INDEX